MONSTERS OF THE SEA

BY "DINO" DON LESSEM

ILLUSTRATED BY
JOHN BINDON

For Lucy—D.L.

For Hall. Thanks for your neverending dinosaur factoids
and insights.—J.B.

Copyright © 2002 by Don Lessem. Illustrations copyright © 2002 by John Bindon. All rights
reserved. Published by Grosset & Dunlap, a division of Penguin Putnam Books for Young
Readers, New York. GROSSET & DUNLAP is a trademark of Penguin Putnam Inc.
Published simultaneously in Canada. Printed in China.

Library of Congress Cataloging-in-Publication Data is available.

ISBN 0-448-42646-3   A B C D E F G H I J

A Word from Dino Don

Did you know that real monsters once swam the seas? At the same time that dinosaurs ruled the land, strange and huge reptiles ruled the oceans. Some of these sea monsters included killers as large and mean as *Tyrannosaurus rex*. Other sea giants had long necks or enormous skulls. Over 170 million years of ocean life, these reptiles developed into many strange creatures, with oddly shaped tails, skulls, and teeth.

Nothing like these monsters lives today, but back when dinosaurs ruled the earth, the sea was full of creatures just like these. Then, 65 million years ago, the last of the giant sea reptiles disappeared. The sea monsters vanished as mysteriously as the dinosaurs did, at the very same time. But new fossil discoveries are now revealing more of the strange giants who once ruled the seas. I think you'll love the weird water giants that you'll meet here—I do!

'Dino' Don Lessem

SEA MONSTERFACT

Today, the largest creature in the world is a sea mammal, the blue whale. But when dinosaurs ruled the land, the kings of the oceans were all reptiles.

DINO DON SAYS: Marine reptiles were NOT dinosaurs, though both were big and scary and they lived at the same time. Reptiles are not the same kind of animals as dinosaurs, and no dinosaur lived in the water. Also, some of these sea giants gave birth to live young. Dinosaurs laid eggs.

GIANT MOTHERS

Strange, fierce, and longer than a school bus, a huge reptile swims powerfully through the ancient sea. As it moves, its body contracts and pushes out something tiny and alive. It's a baby *Shonisaurus* (SHOW-nee-SORE-us).

The *Shonisaurus* mother was one of the largest of all sea creatures. In its time, 210 million years ago, it was the largest animal on Earth, bigger than any dinosaur. But its young were tiny—newborn swimmers might have been just a few feet long.

The early sea reptiles are divided into a few different groups by scientists. *Shonisaurus* was an ichthyosaur (ICK-thee-o-sore), which means "fish lizard." Some ichthyosaurs were just a foot long. But all ichthyosaurs had stiff flippers instead of separate toes. They also had tail fins that bent downward and flapped as the creatures swam like fish.

SEA MONSTERFACTS

Shonisaurus

MEANING OF NAME: "Shoshone Mountains lizard"

GROUP: Ichthyosaur

PLACE: North American West

TIME: Late Triassic Period, 210 million years ago

SIZE: 50 feet and perhaps 80 feet long

DIET: large fish, other marine reptiles

YEAR NAMED: 1976

DINO DON SAYS: Shonisaurus *had blade-shaped ridges on the sides of its teeth, which it used to help snag and slice big fish and other marine reptiles. A Shonisaurus* dentist *would have to be very careful!*

LONG-LEGGED MONSTERS

A long-limbed *Nothosaurus* (NO-tho-SORE-us) chases a turtle-like *Placodus* (PLAK-o-duss) away from its shoreline territory. This time, the Placodus gets away—this is a slow-moving chase compared to the speed of many sea monsters.

Both of these animals were among the first large reptiles in the sea 230 million years ago, before dinosaurs even existed. Nothosaurs were bulky creatures. They resembled long-necked lizards with wide heads and long, spike-shaped teeth that were good for snaring fish. They had webbed feet and swam like otters.

Nothosaurs lasted 30 million years, but they were replaced by faster, sleeker sea reptiles more than 200 million years ago. The stubby placodonts didn't survive for long as a group either.

DINO DON SAYS: Placodus had armor—thick, bony plates down its spine. Its flat teeth could crush hard shells. Maybe it was strong enough to crunch its own armor—not a good idea!

SEA MONSTERFACTS

Nothosaurus
MEANING OF NAME:
"Mongol lizard"
GROUP: Nothosaur
PLACE: Central Europe, North
Africa, Southwest Asia, East Asia
TIME: Middle Triassic,
230 million years ago
SIZE: up to 14 feet long
DIET: fish
YEAR NAMED: 1834

Placodus
MEANING OF NAME:
"plate tooth"
GROUP: Placodont
PLACE: Central Europe
TIME: Middle Triassic,
230 million years ago
SIZE: up to 5 feet long
DIET: shellfish
YEAR NAMED: 1911

WATER WINGS

Liopleurodon (LIE-o-PLOOR-o-don) flies through the water, flapping like a giant penguin in search of fish to wolf down its big jaws. *Liopleurodon* is speeding toward a big fish breakfast!

Liopleurodon was one of the largest pliosaurs. Pliosaurs were short-necked members of the plesiosaur family of sea reptiles. Plesiosaurs appeared when the Jurassic Period began, nearly 200 million years ago. All plesiosaurs had long legs shaped like wings. Their short tails helped them to steer. By the end of the Jurassic Period, 145 million years ago, pliosaurs were the rulers of the sea, dominating ichthyosaurs and the slower-moving long-necked plesiosaurs.

SEA MONSTERFACTS

Liopleurodon

MEANING OF NAME:
"smooth-sided tooth"

GROUP: Plesiosaur

PLACE: Central Europe

TIME: Late Jurassic,
160 million years ago

SIZE: up to 40 feet long

DIET: fish, ichthyosaurs, other
marine reptiles

YEAR NAMED: 1873

DINO DON SAYS: We don't know if plesiosaurs laid eggs on land or gave birth to live young at sea, as ichthyosaurs do. I'm sure plesiosaurs knew the answer, but they're not talking about it.

WATER-TASTING HUNTERS

A huge-headed *Kronosaurus* (KRON-o-SORE-us) darts up through a sea forest of kelp to bite at its rival. Its head is enormous, big and strong enough to bite off the head of any other sea creature. But wait! How did it even see through this underwater jungle?

The *Kronosaurus* could find its way in the dense underwater jungle because it swam with its mouth open. Water went up holes in the roof of its mouth, through smelling tubes, and then out through its nose. In this way, just like sharks today, *Kronosaurus* and other pliosaurs could "smell" other animals in the water!

SEA MONSTERFACTS
Kronosaurus
MEANING OF NAME: "Kronos lizard," for its huge size (Kronus was a Titan giant of legend)
GROUP: Plesiosaur
PLACE: Australia
TIME: Late Cretaceous, 80 million years ago
SIZE: up to 56 feet long
DIET: fish, other marine reptiles
YEAR NAMED: 1924

DINO DON SAYS: Kronosaurus *was a really big meat-head. This hunter had a noggin two feet longer than T. rex's head— that means it was at least eight feet long! I bet it had a hard time finding hats that fit.*

DINO DON SAYS: Tiny, unborn ichthyosaurs have been discovered inside the body cavity of adult ichthyosaur skeletons in Germany. They gave birth like humans do! However, ichthyosaurs didn't nurse their young or have hair, like we and other mammals do. And they didn't diaper their babies, either!

SPEEDSTERS IN THE SEA

Slicing beneath the waves, a pod of *Ichthyosaurus* (ICK-thee-o-SORE-us) chases squid-like cephalopods (SEF-a-lo-PODS). The cephalopods are doomed—nothing in their sea swims faster than the ichthyosaurs.

Most ichthyosaurs were the size and shape of dolphins. They were the fastest swimmers among sea reptiles. But unlike dolphins, who swish their tails up and down to generate speed, ichthyosaurs were powered by the side-to-side movements of their tails. Four paddles helped ichthyosaurs control their direction, even while diving for bottom-swimming fish. A fleshy fin atop their backs also helped stabilize these expert swimmers.

SEA MONSTERFACTS

Ichthyosaurus

MEANING OF NAME: "fish reptile"
GROUP: Ichthyosaur
PLACE: England
TIME: Early Jurassic, 180 million years ago
SIZE: up to 6 feet long
DIET: fish, shellfish, cephalopods
YEAR NAMED: 1818

NIGHT HUNTERS

Night is falling, 150 million years ago, over the shallow sea that covered what is now England. It's hunting time for the big-eyed ichthyosaur *Opthalmosaurus* (OP-thall-mo-SORE-us). This tiger-sized predator is using its superior vision to hunt squid and fish in the dark.

By the time of *Opthalmosaurus*, late in the Jurassic Period, crocodiles, large pliosaurs, and long-necked plesiosaurs were becoming more common. Ichthyosaurs were no longer the rulers of the sea. But *Opthalmosaurus* was still common in this very diverse ocean community.

DINO DON SAYS: Ophthalmosaurus had pointy teeth, all set in a single groove instead of in separate sockets like your teeth or those of most ichthyosaurs. The reasons for this design are a mystery. But it probably made it harder for teeth to fall out. Bad news for the tooth fairy!

SEA MONSTERFACTS

Opthalmosaurus
MEANING OF NAME: "eye lizard"
GROUP: Ichthyosaur
PLACE: England
TIME: Late Jurassic, 150 million years ago
SIZE: up to 11 feet long
DIET: fish, squid
YEAR NAMED: 1874

THE LONG-NECKS

Cryptoclidus (CRIP-toe-CLY-duss) stretches its long neck upward as it darts up from below to surprise small fish. How do we know they hunted in this way? Actually, we don't. But their eyes faced upward and forward, so scientists think they hunted from below their prey, hiding their large bodies.

Using this technique, small plesiosaurs like *Cryptoclidus* were able to ambush their prey. But they had to be on the lookout for ichthyosaurs, which were twice their size. The long-necked plesiosaurs would not reach their largest sizes until the last period in the Age of the Dinosaurs, the Cretaceous.

SEA MONSTERFACTS

Cryptoclidus

MEANING OF NAME: "hidden clavicle" for the location of its wishbone.

GROUP: Plesiosaur

PLACE: Central Europe

TIME: Late Jurassic, 150 million years ago

SIZE: up to 13 feet long

DIET: small fish, squid

YEAR NAMED: 1876

DINO DON SAYS: Plesiosaurs had tiny heads. Even the longest plesiosaur, nearly fifty feet long, had a head no longer than a pony's. That's one big, pea-brained animal!

ROCK-SWALLOWING MONSTERS

A huge *Elasmosaurus* (EE-laz-mo-SORE-us) stretches its long neck to the surface of the water to snap up fish. But just a moment ago, it was eating rocks off the sea floor!

Scientists think that the rocks helped the reptile digest seafood in its gut, in the same way that chickens swallow pebbles to help them break down food in their bellies. Or maybe the elasmosaur's belly stones worked to help it dive deep in search of bottom-dwelling fish and to weigh down the animal on the ocean floor.

As long as a moving truck, more than half of this creature's length was made up of its neck. At least seventy vertebrae supported the elasmosaur's enormous neck. It was the largest of the long-necked variety of plesiosaurs.

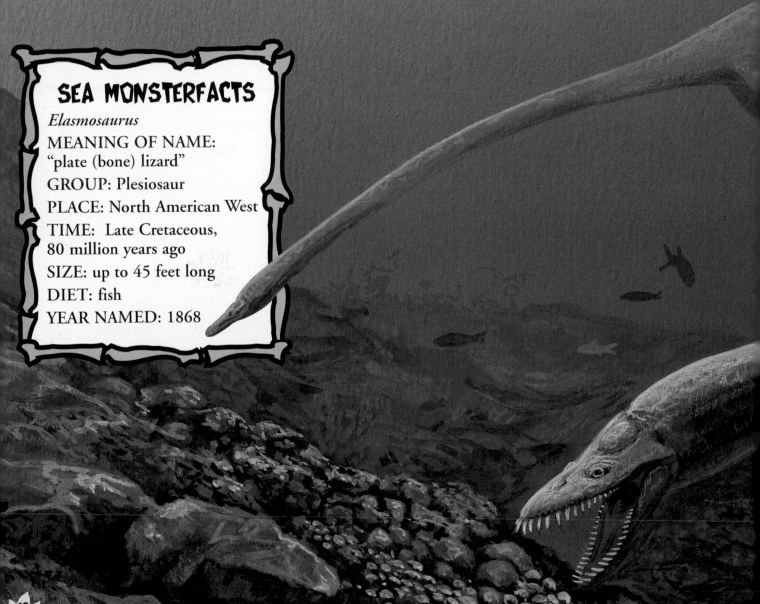

SEA MONSTERFACTS

Elasmosaurus

MEANING OF NAME:
"plate (bone) lizard"

GROUP: Plesiosaur

PLACE: North American West

TIME: Late Cretaceous,
80 million years ago

SIZE: up to 45 feet long

DIET: fish

YEAR NAMED: 1868

DINO DON SAYS: One of history's great scientific goofs was the presentation of the first skeleton of Elasmosaurus. In the late 1800s, Philadelphia fossil collector Edward Cope attached the skull of Elasmosaurus's head on the wrong end of its skeleton!

SWIMMING LIZARDS! THE LAST SEA MONSTERS

Sticking its long snout into the bank of a reef, a *Platecarpus* snaps up a shrimp feast. *Platecarpus* was a mosasaur—a large sea-going lizard with killer jaws. Lizards began on land when dinosaurs did, 230 million years ago. But about 70 million years ago, just before dinosaurs died out, lizards took on some strange new forms. One variety became legless on land—they live on today as snakes. In the sea, lizards grew huge and nasty, with sharp-toothed jaws. Mosasaurs had short legs, webbed toes, and huge tails, so scientists think that they swam like crocodiles.

SEA MONSTERFACTS

Platecarpus

MEANING OF NAME: "oar wrist"

GROUP: Mosasaur

PLACE: American West

TIME: Late Cretaceous, 70 million years ago

SIZE: up to 14 feet long

DIET: fish, birds, shellfish

YEAR NAMED: 1869

DINO DON SAYS: Tylosaurus *was a messy eater—it chewed with its mouth open and swallowed huge hunks of food. It probably didn't use a napkin or a fork, either. Do you want to teach it manners?*

KING OF THE OCEAN LIZARDS

Snapping its long jaws and sharp teeth, a vicious *Tylosaurus* (TIE-lo-SORE-us) leaps up from the water to snare a low-flying pterosaur in its enormous jaws.

A unique hinge in the middle of their lower jaws allowed mosasaurs to open their mouths especially wide so that they could swallow large animals. Fish, pterosaurs, birds, and even other mosasaurs have been found in the belly cavities of large mosasaur skeletons.

Tylosaurus was among the largest of all the mosasaurs. It measured as long as three alligators laid end to end. Only the thickest-shelled animals were safe from tylosaurs. But one mosasaur, *Globidens* (GLOBE-eh-DENS), had teeth shaped like acorns in the back of its mouth. These special teeth helped it crush even thick-shelled animals.

SEA MONSTERFACTS

Tylosaurus

MEANING OF NAME: "knob (snout) lizard"

GROUP: Mosasaur

PLACE: Western North America, New Zealand

TIME: Late Cretaceous, 70 million years ago

SIZE: up to 32 feet long

DIET: fish, pterosaurs, birds

YEAR NAMED: 1872

CROCODILES IN THE DEEP SEA

Far out and deep in the sea 140 million years ago, fish are quietly swimming. Unknown to the fish, danger lurks deep below. A strange, large crocodile, *Geosaurus*, (JEE-o-SORE-us) sits still on the ocean floor. Suddenly, it lunges upward, grabbing and ripping apart fish with its huge teeth.

At the end of the Jurassic Period, two kinds of deep-sea crocodiles appeared, geosaurs and teleosaurs (TEE-lee-o-sores). Teleosaurs had bony plates on their bellies and backs, just like modern crocodiles. But geosaurs did not have armor, so they may have been faster swimmers. Both kinds of ocean crocodiles grew to the size of a large crocodile of today—15 feet long. But the ocean crocodiles had longer and narrower snouts than the shoreline crocodiles of today. A slender head helped these animals to open and shut their mouths quickly to snap up fish in the heavy waves of the ocean.

DINO DON SAYS: Geosaurus *had large, steak-knife style teeth unlike the little, pointy teeth of smaller sea crocodiles. This is one smile no fish wanted to see.*

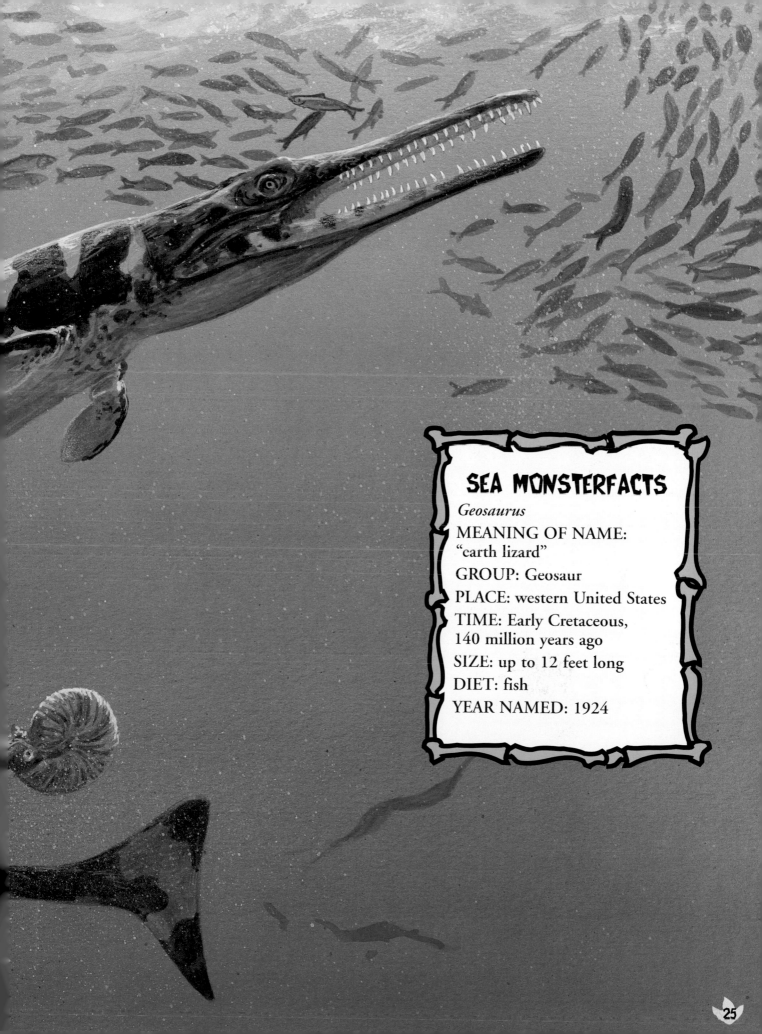

SEA MONSTERFACTS

Geosaurus

MEANING OF NAME:
"earth lizard"

GROUP: Geosaur

PLACE: western United States

TIME: Early Cretaceous,
140 million years ago

SIZE: up to 12 feet long

DIET: fish

YEAR NAMED: 1924

MONSTER TURTLES

A giant sea turtle heads for land. Though it is huge, it swims quickly with its long paddle limbs and lightweight shell. On the shore, it digs, lays its eggs, and buries them in sand. Year after year, it returns to the same place.

Today, sea turtles still lay their eggs each year on beaches around the world. But no sea turtle today ever grows as large as this *Archelon* (ARK-e-lon) did. It was bigger than most bedrooms! Even though they are smaller now, sea turtles are the only deep-ocean reptiles that have survived from the time of dinosaurs.

DINO DON SAYS: Compared to other giants of the Mesozoic seas, Archelon *was a sweetheart. But it still makes me glad I never had to swim in dinosaur times!*

SEA MONSTERFACTS

Archelon

MEANING OF NAME:
"ruler turtle"

GROUP: Chelonian (turtles
and tortoises)

PLACE: North American West

TIME: Late Cretaceous,
70 million years ago

SIZE: up to 12 feet wide

DIET: fish

YEAR NAMED: 1896

A CHILD'S FOSSIL FIND

Would you believe that a young girl made some of the most important discoveries in the history of sea reptile studies? Well, it's true! Her name was Mary Anning, and she lived in England nearly 200 years ago.

Mary was just twelve years old when her brother made the first of several great fossil finds near their seashore home. He had found the skeleton of an ancient sea reptile, an ichthyosaur. Over thirty years of searching, Mary herself found the first fossils of plesiosaurs and flying pterosaurs. At the time, scientists knew very little about the age and forms of ancient life. Mary Anning's finds helped establish the science of paleontology.

DINO DON SAYS: If Mary could find sea monsters, so can you. If you find a fossil, please don't try to dig it out! It won't bite, but it's best to tell a scientist about it and let him or her supervise. Scientists break things too, but not so often as we amateurs do!

Mary's finds helped her support her family for many, many years. They even made her famous. Mary may have inspired a well-known children's tongue twister: "She sells seashells by the seashore."

MODERN MONSTERS

Across the swirling sea, sailors catch a glimpse of a huge oarfish. It's an enormous fish, longer than a school bus! But in the mist, it could easily be mistaken for a giant sea monster.

Are giant sea reptiles still alive? Around large lakes all over the world, from Loch Ness, Scotland to Lake Champlain, New York, local people have claimed to see giant animals in the water. Are these freshwater creatures relatives of the ancient plesiosaurs, as many people believe? There is no proof.

For any sea reptiles to have survived more than 65 million years after the rest of their kind died out would be hard to explain. A population of hundreds of these animals would be needed to keep their kind alive for so long. If these animals truly were alive all that time, chances are that we would have lots of pictures, and maybe even their bones.

But even if sea reptiles live on only in our imaginations, they were once very real and spectacular animals. It's too bad we were not alive to see them swim—from a safe distance!

DINO DON SAYS: Why did the marine reptiles disappear? For some unknown reason, dinosaurs, pterosaurs, giant marine reptiles, and many other animals died out 65 million years ago. Perhaps an asteroid crash changed the weather so they couldn't survive. But it appears many of these animals were already on their way out, perhaps because of slow climate changes.

Marine Reptile Locations for this Book

MESOZOIC ERA millions of years ago

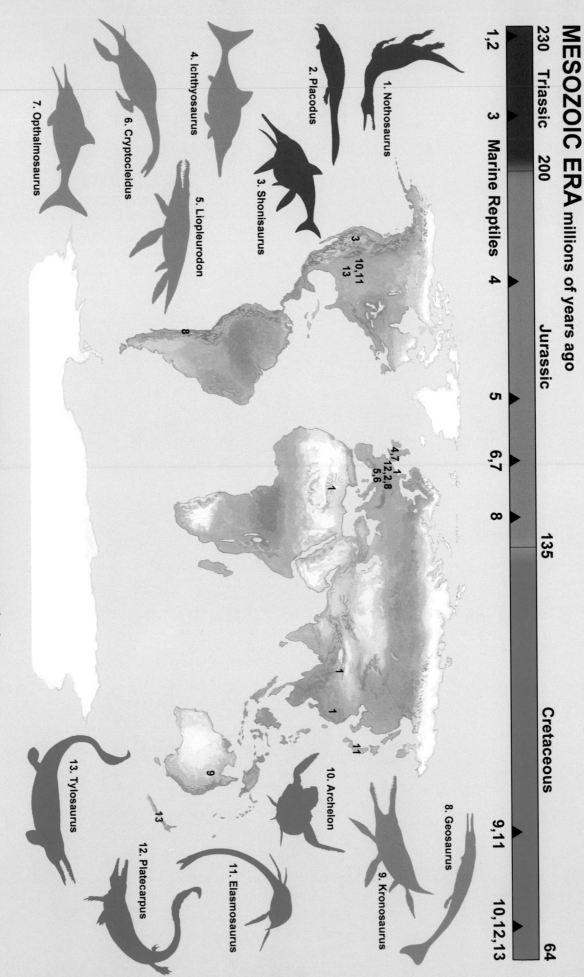

230		200		135		64
Triassic		Jurassic			Cretaceous	

Marine Reptiles

1,2　3　4　5　6,7　8　9,11　10,12,13

1. Nothosaurus
2. Placodus
3. Shonisaurus
4. Ichthyosaurus
5. Liopleurodon
6. Cryptocleidus
7. Opthalmosaurus
8. Geosaurus
9. Kronosaurus
10. Archelon
11. Elasmosaurus
12. Platecarpus
13. Tylosaurus

A WORLD OF SEA MONSTERS

Giant sea creatures lived everywhere there were oceans, all throughout the Age of Dinosaurs. We know of more than one hundred kinds of these ocean giants so far, but hundreds more probably existed. This map shows you where we've found fossils so far of the Mesozoic marine reptiles featured in this book.